SPORTS STARS WITH HEART

Derek Jeter

CAPTAIN ON AND OFF THE FIELD

by Tom Robinson

 Enslow Publishers, Inc.
40 Industrial Road
Box 398
Berkeley Heights, NJ 07922
USA
http://www.enslow.com

Library of Congress Cataloging-in-Publication Data
Robinson, Tom.
  Derek Jeter : captain on and off the field / Tom Robinson. — 1st ed.
    p. cm. — (Sports stars with heart)
Includes bibliographical references and index.
ISBN-13: 978-0-7660-2819-7
ISBN-10: 0-7660-2819-4
1. Jeter, Derek, 1974—-Juvenile literature. 2. Baseball players—United States—
Biography—Juvenile literature. I. Title. II. Series.
  GV865.J48R63 2006
  796.357092—dc22
  [B]   2006012542

Paperback ISBN-13: 978-0-7660-3601-7
Paperback ISBN-10: 0-7660-3601-4

Credits
Editorial Direction: Red Line Editorial, Inc. (Bob Temple)
Editor: Sue Green
Designer: Lindaanne Donohoe

Printed in the United States of America

10 9 8 7 6 5

To Our Readers: We have done our best to make sure all Internet addresses
in this book were active and appropriate when we went to press. However, the
author and the publisher have no control over and assume no liability for the
material available on those Internet sites or on other Web sites they may link to.
Any comments or suggestions can be sent by e-mail to comments@enslow.com
or to the address on the back cover.

♻ Enslow Publishers, Inc., is committed to printing our books on recycled paper. The paper
in every book contains 10% to 30% post-consumer waste (PCW). The cover board on the
outside of each book contains 100% PCW. Our goal is to do our part to help young people
and the environment too!

Photographs © 2006: AP Photo: 38; AP Photo/Roberto Borea: 3, 25;
AP Photo/Robert F. Bukaty: 4; AP Photo/Gregory Bull: 108; AP Photo/Chris Carlson:
111; AP Photo/Richard Drew: 102; AP Photo/Frank Franklin II: 88; AP Photo/Ron
Frehm: 53, 63, 102; AP Photo/Bob Galbraith: 97; AP Photo/Julie Jacobson: cover, 1, 3;
AP Photo/Kalamazoo Gazette, Chad Stevens: 3, 17; AP Photo/Rusty Kennedy: 6;
AP Photo/Bill Kostroun: 71, 90; AP Photo/Ron Leifeld: 73; AP Photo/ Mark Lennihan:
31, 37, 45, 61; AP Photo/Suzanne Plunkett: 99; AP Photo/Louis Requena: 54;
AP Photo/Amy Sancetta: 85; AP Photo/Rich Schultz: 13; AP Photo/Pat Sullivan: 66;
AP Photo/Nick Wass: 80; AP Photo/ Kathy Willens: 21

Cover Photo: New York Yankee Derek Jeter slides safely into third base
April 5, 2005, in a game against the Boston Red Sox at Yankee Stadium.

C O N T E N T S

Jeter fields a ground ball at Legends Field in Tampa, Florida.

CHAPTER ONE

Thriving in the Spotlight

The New York Yankees were in trouble. The Yankees already trailed the Oakland Athletics, two games to none, in the 2001 American League Divisional Series, and their 1–0 lead in the seventh inning of Game 3 seemed to be bouncing away.

Shane Spencer's throw from right field got past two cutoff men and was bouncing past the first-base line into foul territory as Oakland's Jeremy Giambi tried to race from first base all the way home with the tying run.

That's when Derek Jeter flashed onto the screen. In the scene that may have been the single most repeated sports highlight of the year, Jeter arrived from his shortstop position on the other side of the

Derek Jeter (left) and Scott Brosius celebrate a win.

infield, caught the ball, and in one continuous motion, shoveled it on to catcher Jorge Posada in time to tag out Giambi.

The Yankees continued on to win the three straight games needed to get past Oakland and went all the way to the seventh game of the World Series before a dramatic loss to the Arizona Diamondbacks prevented them from taking their fifth title in six years.

The next spring, at the 2002 ESPY Awards, Jeter's gem was honored as the Play of the Year.

It could even be the "Play of the Career" for Jeter because of its spectacular nature. But while one could not have rightfully expected a shortstop to end up in the spot from which Jeter had made his spectacular play, the Yankees have long known they can count on their captain when they need him most.

Jeter has become one of the game's biggest stars. He has reached that point by building a reputation both for clutch plays and consistent, reliable professional excellence.

That reliability extends to baseball fans, teammates, and youngsters in three different states. They all know they can turn to Jeter.

As a teenager, Jeter was regarded as the best high school baseball player in the country. He climbed to the top among minor-league baseball players a couple years later and did not stop even after he had reached the top in the Major Leagues.

The New York Yankees may not win the World Series every year. They do, however, keep themselves in contention to finish as baseball's best team each season. The Yankees do this with Jeter as their captain, leading the way with his example both on and off the field.

Jeter took the fame and fortune that went with being the recognized leader of the most famous franchise in American professional sports and put it to good use. Year after year, Jeter expands on the many programs of the Turn 2 Foundation, which he created. Turn 2 is there for youngsters in Kalamazoo,

Michigan, where he grew up; in New York City, where he makes his career; and in Tampa, where Jeter now resides in the off-season. The Turn 2 Foundation encourages children to adopt healthy lifestyles as well as focus on academics and leadership development.

DEREK JETER'S AWARDS

High School Baseball Player of the Year, 1992.

Sporting News Minor League Baseball Player of the Year, 1994.

American League Rookie of the Year, 1996.

Joan Payson Award for community service (New York baseball writers), 1997.

All-Star Game Most Valuable Player, 2000.

World Series Most Valuable Player, 2000.

ESPY Play of the Year, 2002.

The *Sporting News'* Good Guy in Sports Award, 2002.

American League Gold Glove Shortstop, 2004, 2005, 2006.

TIRELESS WORKER

As captain of the Yankees, Jeter has built a reputation for making clutch plays in the most important of games.

While Jeter may be comfortable in the spotlight, those who know him respect him for the work he does when the cameras are not focused on him and there are not 50,000 people waiting to cheer his every move.

Being named the best player in the country while in high school says a lot about an athlete's potential.

Many of the players who receive such recognition do indeed go on to great success in college or as professionals. The early attention, however, is far from a guarantee of success.

Each time Jeter moved up to a new level of competition, he found obstacles in trying to repeat his performance. Through diligent practice habits, he conquered the new challenges and found both personal and team success again.

TEAM LEADER

When teams choose a captain, they do not just look for the most skilled athlete. The Yankees have several candidates for that honor each year, both returning to the team and coming in to fill in where help is needed.

Jeter became the ideal player to fill the role of captain because of the way he works throughout the year. He is always busy trying to find ways to improve his game or—at the very least—maintain his considerable level of excellence.

Making his off-season home in Tampa is just one of the ways Jeter gets better. He chose that as the place to live so he could be near the New York Yankees' training complex. Long before the team reports to spring training in February to prepare for a new season, Jeter is hard at work on physical conditioning and improving areas of his game that may need some work.

Practically everyone who has played the game enjoys the chance to jump into the batting cage and pound baseballs. Hitting the ball can be fun. Jeter is just as likely to find someone to hit ground balls to him until his back and legs are sore and tired, so that he can make ever-so-slight improvements in the parts of his game that sometimes do not receive as much attention.

Yankees manager Joe Torre, or one of the team's many instructors or coaches, will pass along suggestions for how he can improve his play. Jeter will then spend hour after hour repeating the same play until it becomes something he does naturally in the process of a game.

> **"Baseball is a sport where, until you hit 1.000 and make no errors, you always have something to work on."**
>
> **—Derek Jeter**

First baseman Don Mattingly, who was the team's captain when Jeter first came to the Yankees, noticed that every one of his throws to first base seemed to result in a close play. Mattingly realized that his new teammate hurried when he had to but took his time when it seemed like a play was easy.

The veteran approached the rookie player and

explained that Jeter should make all of his throws with authority, developing good habits and avoiding the risk of unnecessarily close plays.

Mattingly never needed to mention it again.

"Two days after we talked about it, he was doing it exactly the way I'd talked about," Mattingly said.[1]

Jeter was elected the American League's Rookie of the Year—its best first-year player—in 1996. He made it clear, however, that he was only beginning to work on his skills as a professional baseball player.

"Baseball is a sport where, until you hit 1.000 and make no errors, you always have something to work on," he said. "My philosophy is that a lot of people can be better than you, but no one should work harder.

HOW TO FIGURE A BATTING AVERAGE

- Derek Jeter routinely bats above .300, generally considered the outstanding level for a batting average.
- Batting averages are determined by dividing hits by at-bats and expressing the result as a decimal carried out three places.
- Hits are how many times a batter hits the ball AND reaches base safely without the help of an error by a fielder.
- At-bats are times that a batter comes to the plate, excluding walks, sacrifices, and sacrifice flies.
- For example, 11 hits in 40 at-bats is 11 divided by 40, or .275.

"My philosophy is that a lot of people can be better than you, but no one should work harder. I work as hard as anybody, and eventually it should pay off."

—Derek Jeter

I work as hard as anybody, and eventually it should pay off."[2]

Hitting 1.000 would mean hitting the ball and reaching base every time, something that no baseball player comes close to doing during the course of a season. But as Jeter shows in his work, until perfection is reached, there is always something more for which to strive. That is where the work out of the limelight is so important.

Jeter's work with his foundation can be described the same way. Many athletes and other famous people use the attention they receive to help

TOP CAREER BATTING AVERAGES WITH THE NEW YORK YANKEES

Babe Ruth	.349
Lou Gehrig	.340
Earle Combs	.325
Joe DiMaggio	.325
Derek Jeter	.317

Jeter awaits a pitch while playing for the Trenton Thunder May 8, 2003.

raise money for worthwhile causes. Others share some of their riches by making significant donations to charities. Any such efforts are obviously commendable. Jeter does both.

Throughout his professional career, he has maintained his commitment to the Turn 2 Foundation. He keeps adding programs within the foundation. Such continued involvement is uncommon from even the most well-meaning of stars.

Jeter puts his name and face with the big fundraising events and, with help from his family, expands the programs. He spends time with many of the kids in the process, and he tries to create programs that will improve the futures of those they touch.

Since its creation in 1996, Turn 2 has awarded more than $5 million in grants to fund scholarships, camps, after-school programs, and initiatives to both treat and prevent substance abuse. The money comes from fund-raisers, including golf tournaments and dinners, and from Jeter's personal donations.

CHAPTER TWO

Family Influence

Eight-year-old Derek Jeter should have been headed to bed. Instead, he decided to head to his parents' bedroom for a talk. It was then and there that Derek informed his parents, Charles and Dorothy Jeter, that his plan in life was to play baseball for the New York Yankees someday.

Derek's parents did not just send their son off to bed. Instead, they patiently listened to his dreams.

Rather than discourage Derek from aiming for such a lofty goal, his mother and father simply set out to make sure their young son knew what he sought. They reminded Derek that just about everyone in the Westwood Little League where he played in Kalamazoo, Michigan, would probably like to be a Major Leaguer.

DEREK JETER
Born: June 26, 1974
in Pequannock, N.J.

Height: 6'3"

Weight: 175 pounds

Bats: Right

Throws: Right

Team: New York Yankees

Position: Shortstop

Education: Graduated from
Kalamazoo Central High
School in Michigan. Attended
University of Michigan for
one semester.

Off the field: Director of the
Turn 2 Foundation

Millions of Little Leaguers around the country would be whittled down into smaller groups as they got older. There would be Little League all-stars. Then, an even smaller group would become high school starters. Only the absolute best of those high school players would be prospects to play professionally.

If Derek would someday live out his dream, he had to be willing to do the work necessary to be the best. Throughout his childhood, Derek's parents set out a strict set of goals and rules for him to follow. Many of the rules and regulations were not just about baseball. The guidelines for Derek were designed to make him a person who was dedicated to achieving goals.

Before he ever signed his first multi-million dollar baseball contract, Derek signed contracts with his parents, agreeing to responsibilities for the year ahead. The contracts covered all of the issues in Derek's

Jeter runs drills with the Western Michigan University softball team during a Turn 2 Foundation event in 2001.

young life—study routines, practice commitments, chores, and how to avoid getting into trouble that could sidetrack his dreams.

Derek received mostly A's as a student. He eventually became a National Honor Society student in high school. He made other sports teams. And, he kept getting better and better at baseball.

The family that guided Derek at the beginning remains a big part of what he does today. The Jeter family makes up the board of directors for the Turn 2 Foundation. Jeter is the president. His father is

DEREK JETER'S FAMILY

Father: Dr. S. Charles Jeter. Charles was a social worker, specializing in alcohol and drug problems, before leaving his practice to become vice president of the Turn 2 Foundation.

Mother: Dorothy (Connors) Jeter. Dorothy worked earlier as an accounting services manager. She now serves as executive director of the Turn 2 Foundation.

Sister: Sharlee Jeter, a younger sister, is Derek's only sibling. She serves as program director for the Turn 2 Foundation.

the vice president. His mother is the executive director. His younger sister, Sharlee Jeter, is the program director.

WHERE IT ALL STARTED

The Jeter family took roots in Frankfurt, Germany, where both of Derek's parents served in the army. Charles Jeter, who is black, and Dorothy Connors, who is white, met when their roommates brought them along on a double date. Interracial dating was strongly frowned upon in the 1970s. So, when the couple decided to marry, they did so quietly back home in Tennessee in 1973.

Charles Jeter's family was from the South, while the Connors family lived in New Jersey. The newly married couple settled in New Jersey, where Derek was born in 1974.

Just as Jeter now splits his home life between New York during the baseball season and Tampa in the off-season, he had two places to feel comfortable as a child. The family moved to Kalamazoo when Derek was four. He spent each summer with his grandparents in New Jersey, until his baseball commitments eventu-

FEELING AT HOME
- Derek Jeter was born in Pequannock, New Jersey, in 1974.
- Moved to Kalamazoo, Michigan in 1978.
- Continued to spend summers in New Jersey through 1986.
- Now lives in New York City during the baseball season.
- Lives and trains in Tampa, Florida, during off-season.

ally made that impossible when he was thirteen. It was during one of those summer stays with his grandparents that Derek first made a trip to Yankee Stadium to watch "his" team.

As the home of Western Michigan University, Kalamazoo drew students and professors from all over the world. This created a culturally diverse city, which in turn helped Derek feel comfortable while growing up. There were, however, times when Derek was faced with cruel treatment from those who had a hard time accepting a biracial person.

"I'm proud of being from Kalamazoo, but, like anywhere in the world, there were some ignorant and insecure people who lived there, and in the twenty years my family was there, we encountered some of both," Jeter wrote in 2000 in *The Life You Imagine,* his best-selling autobiography. "We didn't run into problems every day, but there were some isolated incidents that are hard to forget."[1]

Later in life, Jeter would share a highly publicized dating relationship with Grammy Award-winning singer Mariah Carey. Although he attempts to keep much of his personal life private, Jeter acknowledged that one of their intriguing similarities was that the singer also came from a mixed heritage.[2]

FATHER'S GUIDANCE

Charles Jeter extended his studies at Western Michigan University. He earned a master's in social work and a doctorate in sociology.

Dr. Jeter built a career in substance abuse counseling. That career provided a positive influence when issues of how and why to avoid drugs and alcohol came up at home. It also created a starting point for many of the programs in Derek's Turn 2

DID YOU KNOW?

One of Derek Jeter's Little League coaches was his father, Charles.

Derek Jeter hugs his father, Dr. Charles Jeter, before the start of the Yankees' game against the Chicago Cubs on Father's Day 2005.

Foundation. Dr. Jeter's experiences allowed him to be a vital sounding board when Derek originally came up with the ideas behind his foundation. Helping youngsters avoid drugs and alcohol was the first goal of the organization.

"Derek wants to set a good example. He wants to be a role model. Seeing that, as his father, I'm extremely proud."

–Dr. Charles Jeter

Derek is proud that conversations with his father led him to creating the Turn 2 Foundation. "You dream as a youngster to play professional sports, and I don't think you realize the magnitude of the impact you can have on someone's life," Derek said. "It can be overwhelming."[3]

Watching his son come to that realization has been fulfilling for Dr. Jeter.

"Derek wants to set a good example," he said. "He wants to be a role model. Seeing that, as his father, I'm extremely proud."[4]

CHAPTER THREE

Preparing Early

The Kalamazoo Central High School basketball team trailed Portage Central, 67–65, when Coach Don Jackson called timeout to set up his team's final offensive possession. Only three seconds remained in the game.

Coach Jackson diagrammed a play that would put the outcome of the game in the hands of a sophomore, Derek Jeter. Jackson went over how the team would in-bound the ball from in front of the mid-court line on the left side. He instructed Derek on how to use a screen by a teammate to get open and receive the ball. He told Derek to go for a three-point shot to win the game rather than a two-point basket for the tie and overtime.

Ten years later when Derek, then a professional baseball player, wrote about his memories of one of

"The next time you ask someone to complete an important task, remind him beforehand about how confident you are that he can do it."

—Derek Jeter

his first starring moments as an athlete, he remembered his coach's words. "We're going to win this game," Coach Jackson said. "We can do it."[1]

The coach's positive attitude alone could not win the game. His confidence, however, helped to eliminate the distractions that could have made it more difficult to succeed.

Derek said he will never forget the feeling of that shot leaving his hand on the way to the basket that won the game, 68–67. He also remembers the coach's positive influence.

"The next time you ask someone to complete an important task, remind him beforehand about how confident you are that he can do it," Derek said. "I'll bet you that he will perform that assignment even better than usual because he will know you feel secure doing it. It has to help someone's state of mind. I know it helped mine in that game."[2]

Derek hoped his coach would call on him that day. Making the shot just helped convince him that he wanted to be in such situations. That has never changed. One of baseball's most successful players in what others might consider stressful situations, Derek still hopes to be the one in position to decide a game.

Derek wanted the ball then. He wants the bat in his hands now. Although his athletic concentration turned strictly to baseball after high

Jeter celebrates a home run in Game 4 of the 2001 World Series.

school, the game-winning basketball shot was just one of many preparations for becoming a winner in Major League Baseball.

DID YOU KNOW?

Derek lived right behind Kalamazoo Central High School when he was growing up. All he had to do to find a field to practice on was to walk through his backyard and climb a small fence.

DEREK JETER THE STUDENT

Jeter started his professional baseball career immediately after high school. To do so, he had to pass up a baseball scholarship from the University of Michigan. He went to Michigan for one semester at the end of his rookie season, but as his baseball commitments lengthened, he was unable to return. In addition to being a member of the National Honor Society in high school with a 3.8 grade point average, he received the Kalamazoo Area B'nai B'rith Award for Scholar Athlete.

Learning what is necessary to succeed extends well beyond the athletic arenas.

As Derek's parents hoped, working for straight A's on a report card served two purposes. It prepared Derek as a student in case his baseball dream did not materialize, and it also helped build habits that are part of his professional life.

The work involved in studying is similar to taking batting or fielding practice. Studying and practice do not always produce immediate results. But when it comes time to pass the necessary test, having developed the needed knowledge or skills makes the task go much more smoothly.

SECOND SPORT

There was time for Derek to eventually become a one-sport athlete. That time came immediately after high school ended.

First, however, he pursued other challenges as a teenager. He accepted a significant challenge to cement his status as a three-year starter and all-state honorable mention selection in basketball. Derek progressed to different levels of baseball, but his parents had to seek out a tryout to help him get used to climbing to a new level of basketball.

After moving away from youth soccer, Derek was down from three sports to two. As long as he was going to be a two-sport athlete, he needed to improve

PROMINENT ACTIVE PROFESSIONAL ATHLETES
FROM MICHIGAN HIGH SCHOOLS

Player	Team, Sport	High School
Shane Battier	Memphis Grizzlies, basketball	Detroit Country Day
Derek Lowe	Los Angeles Dodgers, baseball	Dearborn Edsel Ford
John Smoltz	Atlanta Braves, baseball	Lansing Waverly
Chris Webber	Detroit Pistons, basketball	Detroit Country Day

his basketball game to remain a significant player in a competitive area.

Before Derek started high school, his mother encouraged him to try out for the Kazoo Blues AAU basketball team. Although he had the outside shot that would later lead Coach Jackson to trust the outcome of a game to Derek, he needed to show every bit of his desire and hustle to make a traveling team in his second-best sport. Derek succeeded in his tryout and added to his development in sports. He gained experience by getting to play with and against what would become some of the nation's top college basketball recruits of his era. Derek gained confidence from making the basketball team and learned important lessons about how hard work can help achieve goals.

New York Yankees manager Joe Torre cannot just stop the action and design a play to put a postseason baseball game on Derek's shoulders. Torre has to rely on where the Yankees are in the batting order or where an opponent hits the ball in a key situation. One thing is certain, however. Torre feels the same comfort that Coach Jackson possessed when he knows the game is in Derek's hands.

CHAPTER FOUR

Somebody Is Watching

By the time Derek Jeter started his senior year, high school baseball games at Kalamazoo Central were no longer being played in front of just parents, friends, and classmates. When Derek took the field for each game, he was well aware that somebody else was watching.

Professional baseball scouts found their way to Kalamazoo to decide just how much to pursue Derek when he was ready to graduate high school. Although his dream team, the New York Yankees, eventually picked Derek sixth in the June 1992 amateur draft, many other teams were watching.

Teams that would draft ahead of the Yankees had to decide whether they wanted to pick Derek or

Derek Jeter lives his boyhood dream by playing for the New York Yankees.

an older, more-established college player. The Yankees were in the process of making their decision. Even if the Yankees were sure they wanted a high school kid from a northern state with limited opportunities to play in a short season, they were not going to share that information with rival teams. Therefore, teams that picked behind the Yankees were also looking at the shortstop who would finish the season widely recognized as the best high school player in the country.

Every move Derek made was analyzed. The strength of his throwing arm, the amount of ground he covered in the infield, and the speed with which he got down to first base after hitting the ball were all assessed. Stopwatches, radar guns, and the knowing eyes of men who spent their lives in the sport were all trained on Derek in an effort to determine just how likely he was to become a successful professional baseball player.

Derek sprained his ankle early in the season. That only added more questions to the mix. If he sat out too long, teams could worry about the lasting impact of the injury. If he returned too soon at less than full strength, he might not look as impressive. The questions about Derek's future were not simple to address. They were mixed with what was best for him as a high school athlete and what was best for his team.

EARLY PEEK

Yankees scout Dick Groch spotted Derek at a camp when he was a high school sophomore. Groch first noticed the strength of Derek's arm when making throws from shortstop to first base. Soon, Groch saw enough other attributes to know that Derek was something special.

Groch kept a close eye on Derek for the next two years, and the Yankees sent different scouts at times as well. As the 1992 draft approached, the Yankees were serious about Derek. They were looking beyond baseball skills to try to determine how he interacted with team-mates and coaches. What Groch saw was a supremely talented player who loved the game and had fun playing.

"Derek Jeter enjoys playing baseball," Groch said. "He's like a kid at a family picnic. To him, this isn't a job. He's never had a job in his life. He's just play-ing baseball."[1]

> "Derek Jeter enjoys playing baseball. He's like a kid at a family picnic. To him, this isn't a job. He's never had a job in his life. He's just playing baseball."
>
> —Yankees scout Dick Groch

SENIOR YEAR

Derek Jeter's 1992 High School Statistics

At-Bats: 59

Hits: 30

Batting Average: .508

Home Runs: 4

RBIs: 23

Walks: 21

Stolen Bases: 12-for-12

Derek could have fallen back on a scholarship offer to play baseball at the University of Michigan. The presence of so many pro scouts, however, made it clear that Derek was on the verge of getting a chance to immediately turn pro.

The effects of the ankle injury were soon overcome, and Derek was on the way to fulfilling another of the dreams he has shared with his mother. Derek had been reading an article in *USA Today* when he was a freshman. The story detailed why Tyler Houston of Las Vegas had just been selected by the national newspaper as the High School Player of the Year. Derek saved the story, showed it to his mother, and shared another plan. In three years, Derek wanted to win the same award.

Derek moved from the junior varsity to the varsity and into the starting lineup as a freshman. He was clearly one of the team leaders as a sophomore. By the time he hit .557 with 7 homers as a junior, Derek was indeed being considered among the best high school players in the country.

PLAYER OF THE YEAR

The New York Yankees were not the only people who thought Derek Jeter was the best high school player in the country in 1992. Among his awards that year were:

- Gatorade High School Athlete of the Year.
- *USA Today* High School Baseball Player of the Year.
- American Baseball Coaches Association High School Player of the Year.

The ankle injury only briefly slowed his pursuit of top honors. By the time Derek's senior season was over, *USA Today* was just one of many publications that considered him the best high school player in the country. Most important, the New York Yankees and essentially all of organized professional baseball had agreed. No other high school player was selected in the draft prior to the Yankees making Derek the sixth overall pick.

The first sixteen picks in the draft included just one other high school player. The New York Mets chose Preston Wilson from South Carolina with the ninth pick. When the first-round selections were complete, twenty-two college players and six high school players had been chosen.

GETTING STARTED

The college options were still there, but the Yankees were making it clear they wanted Derek. And, as he had been saying since he was eight years old, he wanted to be a Yankee.

All that was left was for the Yankees to make contract offers and for Derek to decide whether to sign. Once he took money as a professional player, he could always attend college, but he would not be able to turn back to play baseball in college.

The monthly pay for players in the low minor leagues is not very high. It is nothing like the contracts famous Major League stars receive. In order to encourage prospects like Derek to sign and begin their professional careers rather than go to college, teams offer signing bonuses. As one of the most sought-after players in the country, Derek would receive one of the largest bonus offers. The Yankees and Derek agreed on a bonus reported to be anywhere from $700,000 to $800,000 on June 28, 1992. *Baseball America* listed Derek's bonus at $700,000, making it tied for the third-highest given out that year.

Baseball America listed Jeter's bonus at $700,000, making it tied for the third-highest given out that year.

The Minor League Player of the Year poses in Yankee Stadium.

Derek hoped to have a week at home to say good-bye to family and friends. After coming up with the money to get him signed, the Yankees told Derek it was time to start his career.

Three days after signing that first contract, Derek arrived in Tampa to play for the Yankees' team in the Gulf Coast League. The Gulf Coast League is a half-season Rookie League. Tampa had already been playing for about two weeks, using players that had signed immediately after the draft in early June. After one day to adjust to his surroundings, Derek was placed in the lineup at shortstop.

New York Yankees shortstop Derek Jeter in 1994

Derek Jeter, Kalamazoo Central star, was now a future New York Yankee. He was still far from taking the infield at Yankee Stadium, but he was ready to embark on a career as a professional baseball player.

Check Out Receipt

Oriole Park

Tuesday, November 16, 2021 4:36:46 PM

Item: R0422194811
Title: Derek Jeter : captain on and off the field
Due: 12/7/2021

Total items: 1

741

5
Moments of Doubt

Baseball can be a frustrating game. In Derek Jeter's first two years as a professional, the game reduced him to tears at times. The phone calls home were often filled with frustration as Jeter, still a teenager, began his professional life.

All types of learning experiences go along with eventually becoming a professional baseball player. Once he arrived at that point, Jeter's newest experience became learning to deal with the increased amount of failure that would be mixed in with his many successes.

The first lessons of Jeter's life as a professional were in dealing with the frustration of striking out. Hitters do not succeed all the time in baseball. One of

"I knew it was going to be an adjustment from high school to pro baseball, but I hadn't expected to feel as overwhelmed as I did. I hadn't imagined that I'd wind up crying in my hotel room night after night because I was playing so poorly."

—Derk Jeter

the most common observations in baseball is that the best hitters—those who bat about .300—"fail" seven out of ten times. They hit the ball well enough to reach base safely just three out of ten times. The nature of the game is such that nobody can get hits all of the time.

Even in high school, teams got Jeter out four or five times out of ten. Most of the time, however, he put the ball in play. He was at least a threat to reach base. In 23 games, he had 59 at-bats and drew 21 more walks (walks do not count as at-bats). In those 80 times up at the plate, he struck out exactly once.

On July 1, 1992, Jeter sat on the bench

for his first day as a pro, but the next day he played shortstop in both games of a doubleheader. When the day ended, he was 0-for-7. He had struck out five times. In the field, he committed an error. Clearly, this was not high school baseball.

"I knew it was going to be an adjustment from high school to pro baseball, but I hadn't expected to feel as overwhelmed as I did," Jeter said. "I hadn't imagined that I'd wind up crying in my hotel room night after night because I was playing so poorly."[1]

Jeter was 0-for-14 before he finally got his first hit almost a week later. When the season was over, he posted the lowest season batting average of his life—.202.

NEW ISSUES

Before long, Jeter got better at the plate. He built his batting average up each year, but his troubles were far from over. Jeter's first full season, starting in April of 1993, brought about the realization that he needed significant work on his defense. The tears and frustration returned while playing at Class A Greensboro.

Shortstops usually make more errors than players at any other position in baseball. This happens despite the fact that most teams put their best players at shortstop. The position is the busiest, except for catcher, and produces the most demanding plays.

As an all-star shortstop with the Yankees, Jeter is

YANKEES FARM SYSTEM

Draft picks and undrafted free agents pass through as many as six levels of the minor-league system, also known as the farm system, on their way to becoming New York Yankees.

Rookie – Gulf Coast Yankees, Tampa

Half-season Class A – Staten Island Yankees

Class A – Tampa Yankees

Class A – Charleston River Dogs (Greensboro when Derek Jeter was a minor-leaguer)

Class AA – Trenton Thunder (Albany when Derek Jeter was a minor-leaguer)

Class AAA – Columbus Clippers

predictable. He has made only 13, 14, or 15 errors in each season from 2001 through 2005. Playing in the shorter minor-league season, Jeter committed 56 errors at Greensboro. Only his parents knew how much Jeter was suffering while wondering what was going wrong. Jeter's early phone bills exceeded $300 a month as he called home and made the most of his father's career in counseling.

"I probably cried at least once about each error," Jeter said. "Cried to my parents; cried myself to sleep. . . . But no one with the Yankees knew how much I was hurting. Only my parents. I don't like to show my emotions to anyone."[2]

DEREK JETER'S ERROR COUNT

After committing 56 errors in 126 games in the minor leagues in 1993, Derek Jeter made himself into a top-notch defensive shortstop with the New York Yankees. His error totals in New York:

Year	Games	Errors
1995	15	2
1996	157	22
1997	159	18
1998	148	9
1999	158	14
2000	148	24
2001	150	15
2002	156	14
2003	118	14
2004	154	13
2005	157	15
2006	150	15
2007	155	18

Jeter would start to make a quality play on defense. Finishing what he started was often his problem. "I was the king of robbing a player of a potential hit and whipping it past first so that the hitter wound up on second," Jeter said.[3]

Confidence is part of what helps Jeter succeed with 50,000 people on their feet and a professional championship at stake. That confidence, however, was eroding with each error.

The Yankees liked that Jeter got to so many ground balls. Many coaches and instructors, even general manager Gene Michael, spent time in Greensboro working with Jeter. They concentrated on improving his footwork so that he would pick up the ball cleanly more often. This would put him in a better position when it came time to make the throw.

Michael, who was known for his fielding skill as the Yankees' shortstop in his playing days, told Jeter that he was fielding each ball differently. He stressed scooping up the same type of grounders the same way each time. "He started to become more careful," Michael said. "He had been a little careless. I think he values the baseball more now."[4]

The improvements in practice slowly rebuilt Jeter's confidence. He repeatedly practiced making the routine plays that had been strikeouts as a Rookie League player or errors as a second-year professional. Once the plays were made repeatedly in game situations, Jeter looked forward to the chance to continue his success in the clutch.

Extra work in the Instructional League with infielder instructor Brian Butterfield after the 1993 season and the thousands of ground balls Jeter took on his own eventually paid off. In 1998, he made just 9 errors in 149 games with the Yankees.

Yankees general manager Gene Michael helped Jeter learn to play each ground ball the same way, to cut down on errors.

Long before Jeter saw the positive results, how-ever, others were seeing the promise. Each step through the minors brought about a new level of competition, but before long, Jeter was showing he could handle it.

DEREK JETER'S MINOR-LEAGUE HIGHLIGHTS

1992: Batted .210 with four homers and 29 RBIs in 58 games at Tampa and Greensboro.

1993: Spent entire season in Greensboro. Made South Atlantic League all-star team. Was second in league with 11 triples. Batted .295 with five homers, 71 RBIs, and 18 stolen bases.

1994: Minor League Player of the Year. Batted .344 with 5 homers, 68 RBIs, and 50 stolen bases while moving from Class A Tampa to Class AA Albany to Class AAA Columbus. Was named Most Valuable Player of the Florida State League for his play in Tampa.

1995: International League All-Star. Batted .317 at Columbus for the best average by any Yankees minor-leaguer.

By the end of the 1993 season, rival managers in the South Atlantic League were seeing the same things that Yankees scout Dick Groch and others had seen when watching Jeter in high school. Despite those 56 errors, the managers voted Jeter as the "Most Outstanding Major League Prospect" in the league.

CHAPTER SIX

On the Rise

Prospect means one thing: the likelihood—or prospect—that a player will become a star. In 1993, South Atlantic League managers thought Derek Jeter was the best Major League prospect in their league. But that was just one league with six Class AA and AAA leagues above it.

Just a year later, Jeter's potential was not an issue. The talk turned to what he was actually accomplishing. When the 1994 season was over, Jeter was universally regarded as the best player in all of the minor leagues. Jeter celebrated his twentieth birthday midway through that season. Suddenly, he was very close to becoming a New York Yankee.

CLIMBING QUICKLY

Jeter played on three levels of the minor leagues in 1994. He started out at Tampa, this time with the full-season Class A team in the Florida State League, not the rookie team. That did not last long.

The season started innocently enough. Jeter batted just .232 in April, but then took off. Jeter scored a run per day in May, topping all minor-league players with 31 runs while hitting .391 to lead all the players in the Yankees' farm system. He wound up being named Florida State League Player of the Month for June even though he was off to Albany and the Class AA Eastern League before the month was over. In the last 49 games he would ever play in Class A, Jeter batted .367 for Tampa, including 5 hits in one game June 10.

The ridiculous numbers just continued at Albany. Class AA often starts the separation process between the prospects who will keep climbing and those who are going to have a hard time making it to the top. Jeter played so well at Albany that the Yankees were not even able to keep him there for six weeks.

Jeter was named Player of the Month again, this time in the Eastern League for July, when he batted .420. He left Albany with a .377 batting average.

By August 1, Jeter was done with Class AA and on his way to the Class AAA Columbus Clippers of the International League, one step away from New York.

"He's legit," Clippers manager Stump Merrill said after less than three weeks as Jeter's manager. "He's got a chance to be something special."[1]

He barely slowed down with the Clippers. He hit .349 in 35 games. The best pitchers in minor-league baseball were never able to hold Jeter without a hit for two straight games. The amazing season had a sparkling finish. Jeter went 4-for-4 in Toledo August 31, part of a season-ending, five-game hitting streak in which he had 11 hits in 19 at-bats.

> **"He's legit. He's got a chance to be something special."**
>
> **—Clippers manager Stump Merrill**

MINOR LEAGUE PLAYER OF THE YEAR

The Sporting News, Baseball America, USA Today Baseball Weekly and Topps/NAPBL all named Derek Jeter Minor League Player of the Year following the 1994 season. He ranked in the top 15 of all minor-leaguers in several statistics:

Category	Total	Rank
Hits	186	2nd
Runs scored	103	10th
Batting average	.344	10th
Stolen bases	50	14th

MAJOR-LEAGUE DEBUT

After everything Jeter accomplished in 1994, the next step was a natural. The Major League debut could not be far away. Jeter started the 1995 season back in Columbus. Less than two months into another impressive minor-league season, he got the call that he dreamed about back in his bedroom in Kalamazoo where Yankees items, including a uniform and cap, were hung on his wall.

On May 28, the Yankees told Jeter that they needed him. He called home and left Columbus to meet the Yankees in Seattle. Pat Kelly was already hurting, and starting shortstop Tony Fernandez was placed on the disabled list May 29 with a strained rib cage muscle. When Jeter joined the team, the Yankees would need him to play shortstop every day.

STARTING YOUNG

When he made his debut May 29, 1995, Derek Jeter was the youngest player in Major League baseball at the time.

Jeter celebrated his twenty-first birthday that season. When the season ended, he was the third-youngest player to have appeared in the Major Leagues.

Jeter spent all of the 1996 season with the New York Yankees. At 22, he was the eighth youngest player to appear in the Major Leagues that season.

Charles Jeter got up at three o'clock the next morning to fly to Seattle to see his son make his Major League debut. Jeter went 0-for-5 in his first game, but with his father again in attendance at the Kingdome the next day, he got his first hit as a Yankee.

DREAM SIDETRACKED

The Yankees were finishing a homestand June 11, and Jeter could not wait for what was next. After the game, the Yankees were flying to Detroit for a series at Tiger Stadium. Jeter would see his family, and his parents told him that more than 100 people were planning to make the 140-mile drive east from Kalamazoo to Detroit to see him play.

That celebration, however, would have to wait. Jeter was called into a Yankee Stadium office after the game and told that he would be returning to Columbus. Although he had done his job as a fill-in, Fernandez was ready to come back from his injury, and Jeter's big-league career would be placed on hold. So would the first chance for many of the people of Michigan to see him play in person as a Yankee.

He finished another successful season in Columbus. He batted .317 for the Clippers and was selected to the International League all-star team. When the Class AAA season ended, he was called back to the Yankees as part of the expanded rosters that teams are allowed to use in September. He got in two

WHAT IS A ROOKIE?

A player is considered to still be a rookie in the Major Leagues if he starts a season with:

- Fewer than 130 at-bats for a position player.
- Fewer than 50 innings for a pitcher.
- Fewer than 45 days on the active rosters, not counting time on the expanded rosters after September 1.

more games for New York while the Yankees were finishing out the season.

ROOKIE OF THE YEAR

After the 1995 season, the Yankees were counting on Jeter to be their starting shortstop for 1996. From top to bottom, Yankees management stuck with that idea through spring training in Florida, and Jeter was with New York when it opened the 1996 season in Cleveland.

"It's an awful tough job to come into," Yankees owner George Steinbrenner said as the team prepared to head north for the season. "But you see, it's like you go around looking, sometimes, for something to be wrong. Every year, I look for Derek Jeter to stumble a little bit and he doesn't stumble. He just seems to dominate. At

The unanimous choice for the American League's Jackie Robinson Rookie of the Year Award smiles during a news conference.

Double-A, we force-fed him and he dominated there. We force-fed him to Columbus and he dominated there. He could be one of those special ones."[2]

Jeter was the first rookie to start at shortstop for the Yankees since Tom Tresh, another American

Jeter jumps over Rich Amaral during a double play.

League Rookie of the Year, in 1962. He lived up to the owner's prediction almost immediately. Providing a hint of his flair for the dramatic, Jeter hit a home run on Opening Day. He added to his growing list of awards when he was named Rookie of the Year, receiving every first-place vote from the Baseball Writers Association of America.

This time around, there would be no more return trips to Columbus. Jeter claimed the Yankees' shortstop job as his own, playing the position for 157 of the team's 162 games. He scored 104 times while batting .314.

The shortstop of the future had arrived for the Yankees, fulfilling a dream that he had carried with him for the last thirteen years.

AMERICAN LEAGUE ROOKIES OF THE YEAR

1949 – Roy Sievers, St. Louis Browns
1950 – Walt Dropo, Boston
1951 – Gil McDougald, New York
1952 – Harry Byrd, Philadelphia A's
1953 – Harvey Kuenn, Detroit
1954 – Bob Grim, New York
1955 – Herb Score, Cleveland
1956 – Luis Aparicio, Chicago
1957 – Tony Kubek, New York
1958 – Albie Pearson, Washington
1959 – Bob Allison, Washington
1960 – Ron Hansen, Baltimore
1961 – Don Schwall, Boston
1962 – Tom Tresh, New York
1963 – Gary Peters, Chicago
1964 – Tony Oliva, Minnesota
1965 – Curt Blefary, Baltimore
1966 – Tommie Agee, Chicago
1967 – Rod Carew, Minnesota
1968 – Stan Bahnsen, New York
1969 – Lou Piniella, Kansas City
1970 – Thurman Munson, New York
1971 – Chris Chambliss, Cleveland
1972 – Carlton Fisk, Boston
1973 – Al Bumbry, Baltimore
1974 – Mike Hargrove, Texas
1975 – Fred Lynn, Boston
1976 – Mark Fidrych, Detroit
1977 – Eddie Murray, Baltimore

1978 – Lou Whitaker, Detroit
1979 – John Castino, Minnesota (tie)
1979 – Alfred Griffin, Toronto (tie)
1980 – Joe Charboneau, Cleveland
1981 – Dave Righetti, New York
1982 – Cal Ripken, Jr., Baltimore
1983 – Ron Kittle, Chicago
1984 – Alvin Davis, Seattle
1985 – Ozzie Guillen, Chicago
1986 – Jose Canseco, Oakland
1987 – Mark McGwire, Oakland
1988 – Walt Weiss, Oakland
1989 – Gregg Olson, Baltimore
1990 – Sandy Alomar Jr., Cleveland
1991 – Chuck Knoblauch, Minnesota
1992 – Pat Listach, Milwaukee
1993 – Tim Salmon, California
1994 – Bob Hamelin, Kansas City
1995 – Marty Cordova, Minnesota
1996 – Derek Jeter, New York
1997 – Nomar Garciaparra, Boston
1998 – Ben Grieve, Oakland
1999 – Carlos Beltran, Kansas City
2000 – Kazuhiro Sasaki, Seattle
2001 – Ichiro Suzuki, Seattle
2002 – Eric Hinske, Toronto
2003 – Angel Berroa, Kansas City
2004 – Bobby Crosby, Oakland
2005 – Huston Street, Oakland
2006 – Justin Verlander, Oakland
2007 – Dustin Pedroia, Boston

CHAPTER SEVEN

Championship Feeling

Derek Jeter won every individual award imaginable on his way to becoming the New York Yankees' shortstop. Once he got there, all that was left was to start adding ultimate team achievements.

Winning championships almost seems routine for the New York Yankees. The Yankees have won the World Series more often than any other three franchises combined.

As strong as the Yankees' reputation is now, after ten straight playoff appearances since 1996, much of that championship routine was just a part of history when Jeter arrived. Before Jeter was officially honored with the Rookie of the Year Award, which was clearly on the way, he had to lead the Yankees into the postseason.

WORLD SERIES TITLES BY TEAM

Team	Total	First Title	Most Recent
New York Yankees	26	1923	2000
St. Louis Cardinals	10	1926	2006
Boston Red Sox	7	1903	2007
New York Giants	5	1905	1954
Philadelphia Athletics	5	1910	1930
Pittsburgh Pirates	5	1909	1979
Los Angeles Dodgers	5	1959	1988
Cincinnati Reds	5	1919	1990

WORLD SERIES TITLES BY FRANCHISE

Team	Total	First Title	Most Recent
New York Yankees	26	1923	2000
Philadelphia/Oakland Athletics	9	1910	1989
St. Louis Cardinals	10	1926	2006
Boston Red Sox	7	1903	2007
Brooklyn/Los Angeles Dodgers	6	1955	1988
New York Giants	5	1905	1954
Pittsburgh Pirates	5	1909	1979
Cincinnati Reds	5	1919	1990

When the Yankees opened the 1996 playoffs, they were without a world championship since 1978. At that time, the Yankees were not necessarily the team that people thought of as the likely champion.

GETTING STARTED

After that 1978 World Championship, only one Yankees team had won a playoff series. The Yankees reached the World Series in 1981 and lost in six games to the Los Angeles Dodgers. The Yankees were swept out of the playoffs by Kansas City in 1980 and lost in five games to Seattle in 1995. In 1979 and from 1982 to 1994, the Yankees were not even a playoff team.

Early in the 1996 playoffs, it was clear that Jeter would be in the middle of determining whether or not the Yankees would be successful. He batted .412 (7-for-17) as New York beat Texas, three games to one, in the American League Divisional Series. The spotlight then found Jeter in the first game of the American League Championship Series.

Jeter has had his share of SportsCenter moments in his career. His frequent starring performances in baseball's biggest games have created a series of highlights that have been seen over and over and analyzed repeatedly through the years.

The first of those plays came about controversially in the first game of the series with the Baltimore Orioles. Jeffrey Maier, a 12-year-old fan, reached over

Tony Tarasco stretches for the ball as Jeffrey Maier deflects it during Game 1 of the American League Championship Series in 1996.

the right-field fence at Yankee Stadium in the eighth inning, interfering with a long drive by Jeter. Maier reached out over the playing field and caught Jeter's fly ball before Tony Tarasco could attempt to make a play on it. Umpire Rich Garcia was in the outfield because of the extra two umpires used for the playoffs, but he did not call interference. The hit was ruled a home run, and the Yankees forced a 4–4 tie despite arguments from the Orioles.

"In my mind, there is no way I would have dropped it," Tarasco said.[1]

The play wound up as fourth on ESPN.com's ranking of the ten worst calls in sports history.

The Yankees took advantage of the play. Bernie Williams hit a home run in the 11th inning for a 5–4 victory. Although Baltimore recovered to win Game 2, New York took the series by winning the next three games.

Jeter again batted over .400 for the series, going 10-for-24 (.417) with 2 doubles and 2 stolen bases. For the first time in 15 years, the fabled Yankees were headed to the World Series.

WORLD CHAMPIONS

The World Series opened at Yankee Stadium, but the Yankees quickly gave up their home-field advantage. The Atlanta Braves ripped New York, 12–1, on 2 homers by nineteen-year-old Andruw Jones. Greg

Jeter drops a hit by Atlanta's Terry Pendleton during the sixth inning of Game 2 of the World Series October 21, 1996, in New York.

Maddux and Mark Wohlers combined on a shutout in a 4–0 Game 2 win, and the Braves headed home with a 2–0 series lead.

Home runs are exciting, but sometimes a team needs to produce runs one base at a time. The Yankees were in need of some kind of boost when they opened Game 3 in Atlanta. When Tim Raines drew a walk to start the game, Yankees manager Joe Torre decided to bunt to move him to second base and into position to score on any solid hit to the outfield. Jeter executed the bunt, and Raines moved down to second. When Bernie Williams followed with a single to center field, Raines scored, and the Yankees had their first lead of the series.

Williams hit a homer and drove in two more runs in what turned into a 5–2 win in Game 3. The Yankees were still behind two games to one in the series. In Game 4, they fell behind 6–0 after five innings, but they started an impressive comeback that produced three straight tight victories and a world title.

Jim Leyritz hit a three-run homer in the eighth inning to tie Game 4, 6–6. The Yankees won, 8–6, on two runs in the 10th inning to tie the series. Only one team had ever come from further behind to win a World Series game. That was back in 1929 when the Philadelphia Athletics scored 10 runs in the seventh inning of Game 4 to defeat the Chicago White Sox, 10–8.

> **"That was the hit that made us believe we were going to win this thing."**
>
> **—Yankees manager Joe Torre**

1996 WORLD SERIES
Game 1 in New York – Braves 12, Yankees 1
Game 2 in New York – Braves 4, Yankees 0
Game 3 in Atlanta – Yankees 5, Braves 2
Game 4 in Atlanta – Yankees 8, Braves 6, 10 innings
Game 5 in Atlanta – Yankees 1, Braves 0
Game 6 in New York – Yankees 3, Braves 2

Leyritz's homer had turned around the series. "That was the hit that made us believe we were going to win this thing," Torre said.[2]

Andy Pettitte and John Wetteland combined on a five-hit shutout in Game 5 as the Yankees won their third straight in Atlanta, 1–0. Pettitte outdueled John Smoltz, who was the Cy Young Award winner as the National League's top pitcher that season.

After the road team won the first five games of the series, the Yankees were back at home with a chance to clinch at Yankee Stadium. The game was played just a day after Frank Torre, Joe's brother, underwent heart transplant surgery. Jeter, working out of the leadoff spot in the batting order, singled to drive in one run and scored another during the third inning as

Jeter greets Cecil Fielder (45), who hit a home run

the Yankees grabbed a 3–0 lead. They held on for a 3–2 win and the series victory. Wetteland wound up saving all four wins by the Yankees and was named Most Valuable Player of the World Series.

After being outscored 16–1 in the first two games of the series, the Yankees were world champions. They joined the 1985 Kansas City Royals and 1986 New York Mets as the only teams to lose the first two games at home and then go on to win a World Series.

"The mood on the plane ride there was embarrassment," Yankees pitcher David Cone said. "We were thoroughly embarrassed. It was like, 'Let's save some face.'"[3]

The win was not easy for the Yankees. As a team, they hit just .216. Jeter was slowed a bit offensively in the World Series, but he still managed 5 hits and 4 walks in six games while batting .250. He got on base enough to score 5 of his team's 18 runs. For the postseason, he finished with a .361 average in 15 games.

When third baseman Charlie Hayes squeezed his glove around a pop-up by Atlanta's Mark Lemke in foul territory for the final out of Game 6, the Yankees began the celebration of their world title. They took a victory lap around Yankee Stadium as a team. A ticker-tape parade through Manhattan continued the celebration before the team broke apart for the off-season.

Jeter and Jim Leyritz rode the subway together the morning of the victory parade. There, they started receiving the appreciation from New Yorkers. "It is surreal to be on a float with three million people surrounding you and thousands of pieces of paper drifting by your eyes each second," Jeter said. "I'll never forget how we felt that day. I wasn't dreaming about parades as a kid, but now I do. Every year."[4]

CHAPTER EIGHT

Turning 2

Baseball was not the only thing on Derek Jeter's mind as the Yankees closed in on securing a spot in the 1996 playoffs. The Jeter family had missed a chance to be together in Detroit in 1995 when Derek was sent down the night before the Yankees traveled to Michigan to play the Tigers. In September 1996, just before a series in Detroit, a visit with his father in a hotel in the Detroit suburbs changed the lives of everyone in Derek's family.

Derek and Charles Jeter needed time to catch up after not seeing each other much that summer while Derek was traveling around the country with the Yankees. They decided to have pizza delivered to their hotel so they could visit in peace and quiet. During that conversation, Derek told his father that he wanted to start a charitable foundation to help kids.

Charles Jeter knew the subject well. A career social worker with a private practice, he peppered his son with questions about his motives and his plans. As they talked, father and son shared ideas on what soon became a project that would bring the whole family together.

For Derek Jeter, the phrase "turning two" has two meanings. It describes one of his signature plays, turning a double play, something he does so smoothly that he received a Gold Glove as the best defensive shortstop in the American League in 2004 and 2005. But it is also Jeter's goal for young people to be able to "turn to" his foundation for guidance and help to avoid drugs and alcohol while it promotes healthy lifestyles. This is why "Turning 2" is also the name he chose for his foundation. The commitment to both meanings remains as Jeter, who also wears the uniform number 2, keeps working on his defense and keeps finding more ways for his foundation to help young people.

FOUNDATION DEBUT

Jeter was inspired by Dave Winfield, his favorite Yankee, when he was a kid. Winfield, one of the game's first big-money free agents, was the first active player to have his own foundation. Winfield helped thousands of kids.

In the fall of 1996, Jeter was a successful young

Jeter receives a Gold Glove Award from Rawlings representative Steve Cohen on April 23, 2005, at Yankee Stadium in New York.

man with a bright future, but he was not yet playing for the multimillion dollar annual contracts he now receives. He was making about $125,000 a year when he committed his time, his efforts, and his money to the Turn 2 Foundation.

TURN 2 MISSION STATEMENT

To create and support signature programs and activities that motivate young people to turn away from drugs and alcohol and "TURN 2" healthy lifestyles. Through these ventures, the foundation strives to create outlets that promote and reward academic excellence, leadership development, and positive behavior. Turn 2's goal is to see the children of these programs grow safely and successfully into adulthood and become the leaders of tomorrow.

Before Jeter became busy with spring training for the next baseball season, the Turn 2 Foundation made its debut. The foundation was officially launched in December of 1996. It made its first public appearance with a sports auction and kickoff dinner February 7, 1997, at the Radisson Plaza Hotel back home in Kalamazoo.

The Turn 2 Foundation's mission statement was unveiled, and with his family's help, Jeter started building the programs that he has expanded over the years.

Charles Jeter gave up his private practice to run the foundation on a daily basis. He became the vice president. "I knew I would be helping a greater number of people," Charles said.[1] Dorothy Jeter now serves as executive director. After school, Sharlee Jeter

Kicking off his Jeter's Leadership Program in 2000

came to work for the family's foundation. Sharlee
serves as program director.

In its first decade, the Turn 2 Foundation would
ultimately raise more than $5 million for a variety of
programs, ranging from drug prevention to baseball
clinics to academic scholarships. From the beginning, however, Jeter and his family made it clear that
the work was about more than just money. "I didn't

"I didn't want to send donations to different schools or charities and hope the money was used properly, I wanted to establish programs that would have a lasting impact, and we're doing that."

—Derek Jeter

want to send donations to different schools or charities and hope the money was used properly," Jeter said. "I wanted to establish programs that would have a lasting impact, and we're doing that."[2]

EXPANDING PROGRAM

The Turn 2 Foundation, which is a non-profit corporation, features an exhausting list of programs centered around the three areas Jeter considers home—the New York Metropolitan area, western Michigan, and the Tampa Bay area. It supports programs that promote healthy lifestyles, academic achievement, and leadership development among youth.

The Jeter's Leaders Program recognizes students for academic achievements, extracurricular activities, and community service. Leaders are responsible for delivering positive messages to their peers. The program emphasizes the Ten Pillars of Leadership Development: communication, responsibility, morality, taking initiative, lead by example, organized, positive attitude, respectful, trustworthy, and healthy.

SIGNATURE PROGRAMS

Turn 2 After School Program

Turn 2 Baseball Clinics

Turn 2 Holiday Kidfest

Turn 2 Us Healthy Lifestyle Program

Turn 2 Endowed Scholarships

Turn 2 Proud To Be Me

Smart Moves

Jeter's Leaders

Staying Smart at "The Bay"

Turn 2 Youth in Action

The Abyssinian Development Corporation administers the Jeter's Leaders Program in the New York City area. The Kalamazoo Regional Chamber of Commerce runs the program in Michigan. Jeter meets with the leaders throughout the year. The Michigan chapter has traveled to the State Democratic Convention to meet with Governor Jennifer Granholm. The New York chapter has visited Washington, D.C. Members of the two programs were brought together in Philadelphia for a summer leadership conference.

Children's Hospital of New York and Public School 128 in Washington Heights serve as partners in the Turn 2 Us, Healthy Lifestyles Program. The goal of the school-based hospital program is to promote healthy lifestyles and self-esteem through educational, preventive, and clinical care efforts that provide services to students and their families.

About 400 children in Harlem, Brooklyn, and the Bronx take part in the Turn 2 After School Program. Daily activities include computer lab, visual arts, drama, dance, and theme-based learning.

Turn 2 Baseball Clinics have been operating in all five boroughs of New York City since 1998. The six-week program includes a field trip to Yankee Stadium. Turn 2 has added a two-week Baseball Leadership Experience to provide a more extensive training camp for those who excelled in the six-week clinics. A leadership forum, based on Jeter's Ten Life Lessons, is part of the program.

Jeter meets with kids at the Turn 2 Holiday Kidfest, an annual program that rewards more than 1,000 children for leading healthy lifestyles. The event includes baseball contests, food, carnival games, and dancing.

The Turn 2 Endowed Scholarship Program makes three scholarships available to students based on academic achievement and leading healthy lifestyles. The endowed scholarships are the Derek Jeter/Jackie Robinson Foundation Scholarship, the Derek Jeter/ Kalamazoo Community Foundation Scholarship, and the Derek Jeter/Sonny Connors Scholarship. Sonny Connors, Jeter's grandfather, passed away in 1999.

The Turn 2 Proud to Be Me and Turn 2 Smart Moves Programs are based in Kalamazoo. The programs try to help students withstand the pressures of drugs and alcohol and attempt to teach kids the skills needed to say "no" to risk-taking behavior.

The Turn 2 Staying Smart at "The Bay" Program in Bronx, N.Y., is based through a Boys & Girls Club, just as the Smart Moves Program is in Michigan. Participants, ages 10-18, hear from police and probation officers about the legal consequences of drug use. Field trips are designed to illustrate the benefits of making responsible decisions.

Growth of the foundation's list of programs continues. The Turn 2 Youth In Action Program was added in 2005 at the Maple Street Magnet School for the Arts. The program for seventh- and eighth-graders focuses on increasing student achievement. It seeks to motivate students to attend and participate in school. The program develops mentor relationships between youth participants and positive adult role models.

The Jeter Meter is another recent addition. Thousands of students in New York City schools participate in the program, which promotes physical fitness. Students use Jeter Meter cards to track their progress as they run or walk a minimum of one-half mile three to five times per week and try to reach 105 miles during the school year. Once the goals are reached, prizes are awarded. Classes and schools with the most miles receive additional prizes.

There are annual dinners and parties to showcase the various signature programs. The foundation also makes grants to other charitable programs that have similar ideals. An annual celebrity golf tournament in Tampa and fund-raising dinners help raise money to support the Turn 2 Foundation.

The impact Jeter set out to create on the lives of young people clearly has materialized. The dreams that were shared over pizza by father and son have become a reality.

TURNING TWO ON THE FIELD

The goals are separate. Jeter's incredible drive keeps him at the top in baseball. A similar commitment makes sure his grand plans in the charity world become more than just ideas. The two, however, have more of a connection than the simple fact that each shows Jeter's dedication.

One of the reasons that the Turn 2 Foundation has been able to enjoy so much success is the attention Jeter receives. Ongoing excellence on the baseball field keeps Jeter's name in headlines and his face on television screens. That presence makes it easier for him to draw other celebrities to his golf tournament. It creates an extra draw to the Turn 2 Foundation.

Jeter keeps "turning two" on the baseball diamond. It is hard to improve on the lofty levels of success he established early in his career, but turning two is one area where the numbers show Jeter has clearly improved. After never being involved in more than 86 double plays in any of his first eight full seasons, Jeter turned 96 double plays each in the 2004 and 2005 seasons.

Jeter's range factor, which measures the total number of plays he makes in a nine-inning game, also reached new highs in each of those two seasons. As a result, Jeter won two straight Gold Gloves as the best fielding shortstop in the American League.

"Winning the Gold Glove, for the second consecutive season, is extremely gratifying," Jeter said. "Defense usually doesn't make many headlines, but it goes a long way toward winning baseball games.

DEREK JETER'S DOUBLE PLAYS

Year	Games	DP
1995	15	7
1996	157	83
1997	159	87
1998	148	82
1999	158	86
2000	148	78
2001	150	68
2002	156	69
2003	118	51
2004	154	96
2005	157	96
2006	150	81
2007	155	104

Jeter readies a throw to complete a double play in Baltimore.

"There are a number of ways to make an impact during the course of a game, and playing solid, sound defense is one of them. To be recognized with a Gold Glove—with so many other worthy shortstops in our league—is an accomplishment I hold with great honor."[3]

THE YANKEES' MULTIPLE GOLD GLOVE WINNERS

Player	Position	Total	Years
Don Mattingly	First Base	9	1985–89, 1991–94
Dave Winfield	Outfield	5	1982–85, 1987
Ron Guidry	Pitcher	5	1982–86
Bobby Richardson	Second Base	5	1961–65
Bobby Shantz	Pitcher	4	1957–60
Bernie Williams	Outfield	4	1997–2000
Thurman Munson	Catcher	3	1973–75
Joe Pepitone	First Base	3	1965–66, 1969
Derek Jeter	Shortstop	2	2004–06
Mike Mussina	Pitcher	2	2001, 2003
Wade Boggs	Third Base	2	1994–95
Graig Nettles	Third Base	2	1977–78
Elston Howard	Catcher	2	1963–64

Mr. Clutch

New York was back as the unquestioned center of the baseball universe in October of 2000. Sure, Yankees fans might argue that the game always revolves around what happens at Yankee Stadium. But when it is time for a Subway Series, all eyes in baseball turn to New York.

The Subway Series was commonplace in the late 1940s and early 1950s, when New York City was the home of three potent Major League franchises. Seven out of ten World Series between 1947 and 1956 featured two New York teams. The Yankees played the Brooklyn Dodgers in six of those series and the New York Giants in one before those franchises moved to California.

More than four decades had passed since the previous Subway Series. The New York Mets began play in 1962, and the team from Queens had been to three World Series in its first 38 years, but none were against the rival Yankees from the Bronx.

Now, New York City baseball fans had the showdown for which they had been waiting. The Mets were threatening to make things interesting. The Yankees, after sweeping the 1998 and 1999 World Series, started out with two wins against the Mets.

Then, the Mets took Game 3 to end the Yankees' record streak of fourteen straight wins in World Series games. The streak had started back in Jeter's rookie year of 1996 when the Yankees won four straight to overcome a 2–0 deficit.

The Mets were at home at Shea Stadium with a chance to even the series in Game 4. Suddenly, there was suspense. It was a perfect time for Jeter to show his leadership skills

As the visiting team, the Yankees batted first. When manager Joe Torre made out his lineup, he put Jeter in the leadoff spot. Jeter immediately put the Yankees back in the spot they were comfortable in— leading a World Series game. He hit a home run on the game's very first pitch, and the Yankees never trailed. They won, 3–2, to take a three-games-to-one lead in the series.

The Yankees needed just one more win to take the series and become the first team in more than a quarter century to win three straight world championships. The Mets took a 2–1 lead into the sixth inning of Game 5. But Jeter homered for the second straight game, hitting a solo shot with one out to tie the game.

The Yankees never trailed again. They went on to win Game 5, 4–2. For his timely homers in the last two games and producing at least a hit and a run in every game of the series, Jeter was selected as the Most Valuable Player of the World Series.

> **"We made it look easy in three out of the last four years, but this one was a little bit of a struggle for us."**
>
> **—Derek Jeter**

"We made it look easy in three out of the last four years," Jeter said, "but this one was a little bit of a struggle for us."[1]

The Yankees won three games by a single run, including one in extra innings. They did not take the lead in their clinching two-run victory until the ninth inning. Clearly, it was not easy.

Jeter has traditionally been at his best in such settings. His total of 142 hits in postseason games—the American League Divisional and Championship Series and the World Series—is the most in baseball history. Long-time teammate Bernie Williams is the only other

Jeter raises four fingers to signify his four World Series championships.

player with more than one hundred postseason hits.

There is an advantage for Jeter and Williams because they have played in an era where there is an additional round of playoffs. There are two more rounds now than in the playoffs held before 1969.

ALL-TIME POSTSEASON RANKINGS

Where Derek Jeter ranks on the lists of career statistical leaders in World Series and the postseason as a whole:

Statistic	Total	Ranking	Leader
Hits, Postseason	150	1st	Derek Jeter
Runs Scored, Postseason	85	1st	Derek Jeter
Total Bases, Postseason	229	1st	Derek Jeter
Doubles, Postseason	22	2nd	Bernie Williams, 29
Runs Batted In (RBIs), Postseason	48	Tie, 4th	Bernie Williams, 80
Walks, Postseason	51	6th	Chipper Jones, 72
Runs Scored, World Series	27	Tie, 5th	Mickey Mantle, 42
Home Runs, Postseason	17	5th	Bernie Williams, 22
Stolen Bases, Postseason	16	6th	Rickey Henderson, 33
Triples, Postseason	3	Tie, 10th	George Brett, 5

But additional opportunities are not the only explanation. The World Series has been the same for most of the century that it has been around. Jeter ranks fifth in World Series history with 27 runs scored. Every other player in the top 10 has more plate appearances than Jeter because of longer careers.

IN THE SPOTLIGHT

Jeter's reliable, day-in, day-out efforts deserve credit, but he clearly has a knack for performing on the biggest stages. The home run in his first Opening Day as Yankees shortstop is one example. He also had a pair of 3-for-3 performances in the All-Star Game. The first made him the MVP of that contest in 2000, the same year that he was named MVP of the World Series. From that game through 2004, Jeter was 7-for-8 batting in the All-Star Game.

There are other big games besides All-Star Games and the playoffs. For the Yankees, any interleague match-up with the Mets would qualify. Games against the long-time American League East Division rival Boston Red Sox tend to be even more intense.

Perhaps that intensity can explain the cuts on Jeter's head that are part of another frequently repeated highlight. The Yankees and the eventual World Series champion Red Sox were tied in the 12th inning of a game July 1, 2004. Boston's Trot Nixon hit a foul pop-up down the left-field line. Jeter turned his back to the infield, and looked up as he sprinted toward the wall. He made the one-handed catch as he hit the wall at full speed, sending him tumbling into the stands headfirst. Jeter quickly jumped up displaying the ball—for the umpires to see—as well as cuts on his chin and cheek. He went

Jeter dives into the crowd at Yankee Stadium to catch a fly ball in the 12th inning against the Boston Red Sox on July 1, 2004.

to the hospital to have X-rays, but when it was determined that he only had bruises and cuts, he was back in the lineup the next night.

POSTSEASON PERFORMER

If former Yankee Reggie Jackson was not already known as "Mr. October," the nickname might have gone to Jeter. Some of his most famous plays have come in the tensest moments. He says he loves playing when the stakes are at their highest and wants to be the one batting or fielding the ball when championships are being decided. With Jeter leading the way, the Yankees won the World Series four times in his first five seasons.

Jackson was one of the stars when the Oakland Athletics won the World Series in 1972, 1973, and 1974—the last streak of three straight before the Yankees in 1998, 1999, and 2000. Jackson later moved to the Yankees, where he set records with 3 home runs in one World Series game and 5 for the series in 1977, earning him the Mr. October nickname.

Jeter hit a game-winning, 10th-inning homer against the Arizona Diamondbacks in Game 4 of the 2001 World Series. The game started on October 31, but by the time Jeter hit his home run, it was four minutes past midnight. The nickname "Mr. November" made its way into more than a few of the stories recapping the win.

Jeter connects on a game-winning home run October 31, 2001.

During Jeter's career, the Yankees have actually produced a higher winning percentage in the playoffs against baseball's best teams than they have playing a regular-season schedule. They have been to eleven straight playoffs overall. Ten of those playoff trips have come with Jeter on the roster, including nine as division champion. The Yankees are 74–41 in playoff games and have won seventeen of twenty-three post-season series in Jeter's career. In fifteen of those twenty-three series, Jeter has produced a batting average of .300 or better.

THE BEST EVER?

Major League Baseball has been around since the 1800s, but no team has ever won more total games than the 125 produced by the 1998 Yankees on their way to a second world championship in three years. The Yankees jumped out to a 37–13 start in the first two months and won the East Division easily with 114 regular-season victories.

The Yankees were known for their balance. Jeter, in just his third season, was often regarded as the team's biggest star, but none of the Yankees earned an All-Star Game start in voting by the fans.

Dominance continued into the playoffs, where the Yankees swept the Texas Rangers in three games in the AL Divisional Series. The Cleveland Indians caused the only trouble, winning two of the first three

YANKEES PLAYOFF RECORD IN DEREK JETER ERA

American League Divisional Series games	27–19	.587
American League Divisional Series	7–4	.636
American League Championship Series games	27–14	.659
American League Championship Series	6–1	.857
World Series games	21–11	.656
World Series	4–2	.667
All postseason games	75–44	.630
All postseason series	17–7	.708

games in the best-of-seven AL Championship Series. The Yankees won seven straight from that point to become world champions.

Jeter started slowly in the playoffs but was his usual self at the plate in the World Series as the Yankees swept the San Diego Padres in four games.

The Yankees hit 6 home runs in the series, including two clutch shots that put them on the verge of the sweep going into Game 4 on October 21 at Qualcomm Stadium in San Diego. Tino Martinez hit a grand slam in the seventh inning of Game 1. The Yankees scored 7 runs in the inning to overcome a 5–2 deficit on the way to a 9–6 victory.

Scott Brosius, who was named MVP of the series, hit a three-run homer in the eighth inning to decide Game 3, 5–4.

Jeter already had at least one hit in each of the first three games before leading the offense in the clinching victory. Andy Pettitte of the Yankees and Kevin Brown had matched shutout innings when Jeter came to the plate with one out in the top of the sixth. Jeter beat out an infield single, took third on a Paul O'Neill double, and scored the game's first run on a groundout by Bernie Williams.

The score stayed at 1–0 until the eighth inning, when Jeter led off. He drew a walk and scored again. He wound up with the first two runs of the 3–0 victory.

When it was over, the 1998 team had earned a spot in the debate about which was the best Yankees team ever. The team was being compared with the 1927 powerhouse that was led by Babe Ruth and Lou Gehrig and the 1961 team, which got 61 home runs from Roger Maris and 54 more from Mickey Mantle.

BACK-TO-BACK

While winning their third world title in four seasons, the Yankees almost made it look routine.

The 1999 Yankees started the playoffs with a three-game sweep of the Texas Rangers, again. They won all four games in the World Series, again. Jeter got a hit in each World Series game, again. When they

1998 WORLD SERIES
Game 1 in New York – Yankees 9, Padres 6
Game 2 in New York – Yankees 9, Padres 3
Game 3 in San Diego – Yankees 5, Padres 4
Game 4 in San Diego – Yankees 3, Padres 0

needed a big hit, they got it. Chad Curtis hit a game-winning homer in the 10th inning of a 6–5 victory in Game 3.

"They ought to be in a higher league some-where," Atlanta pitcher John Smoltz said after striking out 11 only to lose the fourth and deciding game, 4–1, of the 1999 World Series.[2]

The Yankees lost just one game in the entire play-offs, as Jeter batted .375. After that one loss to Boston, the Yankees won the series in five games. Jeter hit a homer in the 6–1 win against the Red Sox that sent the Yankees back to the World Series.

Jeter went 8-for-18 (.444) when the Yankees swept Texas. He was 7-for-20 (.350) in the five-game league championship series with Boston. He had 2

THE SPORTING NEWS TOP BASEBALL TEAMS OF ALL TIME

A panel of editors from *The Sporting News* selected the best teams of all-time following the 1998 World Series.

1. The 1927 New York Yankees

2. The 1976 Cincinnati Reds

3. The 1929 Oakland Athletics

4. The 1961 New York Yankees

5. The 1978 New York Yankees

hits in each of the first two World Series games and finished 6-for-17 (.353) with 4 runs against Atlanta.

THREE IN A ROW

Jeter again homered in the game that put the Yankees in the 2000 World Series. This time, he hit a three-run shot and David Justice had a two-run blast to back a one-hit shutout in which Roger Clemens struck out 15 Seattle Mariners. The 5–0 victory completed a 4–2 series win.

Getting back to the World Series, however, was not easy this time. The Yankees stumbled to the finish with 15 losses in their last 18 games. They went just 87–74 but took advantage of a down year in the

1999 WORLD SERIES
Game 1 in Atlanta – Yankees 9, Braves 1
Game 2 in Atlanta – Yankees 7, Braves 2
Game 3 in New York – Yankees 6, Braves 5, 10 innings
Game 4 in New York – Yankees 4, Braves 1

AL East. The Yankees faced a possible elimination game for the first time in three years but beat the Oakland Athletics in a Divisional Series that went the full five games.

"A lot of people were trying to say that our run was over, but you're not going to beat us that easily," Jeter said. "We're still the champs until someone beats us."[3]

The first two games of the World Series were far from easy for the Yankees. A series of base-running blunders by the Mets gave the Yankees a chance to stay in Game 1. The Yankees tied the game in the bottom of the ninth and won it, 4–3, in the 12th.

Jeter went 3-for-5 in Game 2, when the Yankees took a 6–0 lead into the ninth and held on for a 6–5 victory.

The two-game edge was cut to one in a rare late-inning playoff loss by the Yankees. The Mets tied the

Jeter watches his home run sail away October 14, 2000.

"A lot of people were trying to say that our run was over, but you're not going to beat us that easily. We're still the champs until someone beats us."

—Derek Jeter

game in the sixth inning and won it, 4–2, with two runs in the eighth. In the loss, Jeter had 2 more hits. He was just getting started. The 2 homers allowed him to finish yet another World Series with a hit in each game. Jeter went 9-for-22 (.407) in the series, scored 6 times, and added 2 doubles, a triple, and 3 walks to his 2 homers while claiming the MVP award.

The Yankees had matched the three straight titles of the 1972–74

2000 WORLD SERIES

Game 1 at Yankee Stadium – Yankees 4, Mets 3, 12 innings

Game 2 at Yankee Stadium – Yankees 6, Mets 5

Game 3 at Shea Stadium – Mets 4, Yankees 2

Game 4 at Shea Stadium – Yankees 3, Mets 2

Game 5 at Shea Stadium – Yankees 4, Mets 2

Jeter accepts the Outstanding Achievement Award in 2000.

> **"This kid [Jeter] right now—the tougher the situation, the more fire gets in his eyes. You don't teach that. It's something you have to be born with."**
>
> **—Yankees manager Joe Torre**

Athletics and added the extra accomplishment of four titles in five years. In a career filled with starring performances, none has been bigger than being named MVP of the first Subway Series in 44 years.

"This kid right now—the tougher the situation, the more fire gets in his eyes," Torre said. "You don't teach that. It's something you have to be born with."[4]

CHAPTER TEN

The Captain

The New York Yankees were struggling through a road trip in the first week of June 2003 when they headed for Cincinnati. George Steinbrenner was not with the Yankees, but the owner is known to stay in close contact with the team's operations, particularly when times are tough. Steinbrenner reached Derek Jeter by phone and let the shortstop know that it was time to take over as captain of the team.

The Yankees had gone more than seven years, the third-longest stretch in team history, without a captain. Although there had frequently been speculation that Jeter could fill the role someday, Steinbrenner had withheld such an appointment until that time.

"It's not something thrown around lightly in the organization," Jeter said at a press conference in

Jeter greets Joe Torre (left) and George Steinbrenner at a rally honoring the team.

Cincinnati, where the Yankees made the announcement on June 3.[1]

Indeed, according to the Yankees, only ten other men had been honored with the assignment in the team history. At least one other baseball researcher believes that four more men may have carried the title in the early 1900s. What was not in dispute is that Jeter would be just the tenth man since 1914 to be named captain of the most successful franchise in American professional sports.

Steinbrenner kept the naming of captain as one of his responsibilities as owner, rather than leaving it up to the manager or general manager. When the team looked sloppy earlier on the 2003 road trip,

**NEW YORK YANKEE CAPTAINS,
1914–2005**

Hal Chase	1912
Roger Peckinpaugh	1914–1921
Babe Ruth	1922
Everett Scott	1922–1925
Lou Gehrig	1935–1941
Thurman Munson	1976–1979
Graig Nettles	1982–1984
*Willie Randolph	1986–1989
*Ron Guidry	1986–1989
Don Mattingly	1991–1995
Derek Jeter	2003–present

*co-captains

Steinbrenner decided it was time. "It was something in the pit of my stomach that said that this was the time," Steinbrenner said. "I also wanted to give the team a message to calm down. I wanted to throw something out there to get their minds on something else."[2]

In their phone conversation, Steinbrenner told Jeter to keep being the kind of leader he always had been. Manager Joe Torre said other players responded to Jeter even back when he was a rookie. "When he first came here, the other players seemed to gravitate

> **"When he [Jeter] first came here, the other players seemed to gravitate toward him, so I thought this day would come eventually."**
>
> **—Yankees manager Joe Torre**

toward him," Torre said. "So I thought this day would come eventually."[3]

Torre acknowledged occasionally talking to Jeter to gauge the "temperature of the club."[4]

When he took the field in Cincinnati, Jeter had an additional responsibility. For the first time since being named co-captain of the basketball team back at Kalamazoo Central High School, he was asked to take a more formal leadership role.

FALL CLASSIC

Since winning the World Series in 2000, the Yankees had continued to reach the playoffs each year but had fallen short of their ultimate goal. The 2001 season had resulted in Jeter's fifth trip to the World Series. The Yankees

Jeter is mobbed after hitting the game-winning home run in the 10th inning of Game 4 of the World Series October 31, 2001.

became the first team to win a divisional series after losing the first two games at home. In the decisive 5–3 victory, Jeter got 2 hits to pass Pete Rose as baseball's all-time leader in playoff hits.

2001 WORLD SERIES

Game 1 in Arizona – Diamondbacks 9, Yankees 1

Game 2 in Arizona – Diamondbacks 4, Yankees 0

Game 3 in New York – Yankees 2, Diamondbacks 1

Game 4 in New York – Yankees 4, Diamondbacks 3

Game 5 in New York – Yankees 3, Diamondbacks 2

Game 6 in Arizona – Diamondbacks 15, Yankees 2

Game 7 in Arizona – Diamondbacks 3, Yankees 2

His streak of getting a hit in fourteen straight World Series games, the third-longest in history, ended in the first game of the 2001 series.

With the playoffs starting late that year because of the interruption of the season following the 9/11 terrorist attacks, Jeter had his "Mr. November" moment with his game-winning home run in Game 4 of the World Series. Playing in their first Game 7 since 1964, the Yankees lost to the Arizona Diamondbacks, 3–2, on two runs in the bottom of the ninth. Luis Gonzalez delivered the winning hit for the Diamondbacks.

The Yankees were eliminated by the Anaheim Angels in just four games in the first round of the 2002 playoffs. Then there was the sloppy play early in

2003. Any question that the team was slipping, however, was answered when the Yankees beat the Boston Red Sox in seven games and returned to the World Series in 2003. It was Jeter's sixth World Series but his first as captain.

Jeter hit .425 in July of 2003, the month after being named captain, to turn the team around and get the Yankees back on their way to the World Series. They led, two games to one, before the Florida Marlins won three straight to take the series.

DID YOU KNOW?

Before losing in Game 7 of the 2001 World Series, the Yankees had won fourteen out of their first fifteen postseason series in Derek Jeter's career.

2003 WORLD SERIES

Game 1 in New York – Marlins 3, Yankees 2

Game 2 in New York – Yankees 6, Marlins 1

Game 3 in Florida – Yankees 6, Marlins 1

Game 4 in Florida – Marlins 4, Yankees 3

Game 5 in Florida – Marlins 6, Yankees 4

Game 6 in New York – Marlins 2, Yankees 0

Jeter starts a double play against Detroit in 2005.

ALL-TIME LEADER

How did Jeter end up in an honored position that had belonged to such greats as Lou Gehrig, Thurman Munson, and, most recently, former teammate Don Mattingly? It might be because of the examples he sets on and off the field. Or, perhaps it is the consistency of his performances through the long 162-game regular seasons and pressure-packed playoffs. More likely, it is the impressive combination of both.

Jeter has hit home runs on the first pitch and the last pitch of big games. He has also shown the willingness to concentrate and hustle on the pitches that come in between.

By the standards of virtually any other team, the 2001 through 2005 seasons posted by the Yankees would be resounding successes. The Yankees kept going back to the playoffs each year. In two of the seasons, they finished up at the World Series, once in a series that was decided in the final inning of Game 7. Another time, they lost a seven-game American League Championship Series.

The Yankees, however, keep striving to be the best. Steinbrenner angers others in the sport by seemingly spending whatever money necessary to get the players he needs. In turn, he demands excellence from those players. It is no wonder then that he would choose Jeter to be the captain.

Jeter has surpassed the magic mark of 200 hits in

a season six times in his career. Only Gehrig, who hit the mark eight times, produced more for the Yankees. Over the first ten full seasons of Jeter's Major League career (1996–2005), nobody in baseball produced as many hits (1,924), and only one man scored more runs (1,154).

As the 2005 season was winding down, Jeter played in the 1,500th game of his career September 6 against Tampa Bay. At that point in his career, he had 1,906 hits and 1,140 runs. The last player in the Major Leagues with as many hits and runs at that point in his career was another Yankee great, Joe DiMaggio, the man who holds baseball's record for getting hits in fifty-six straight games.

Jeter's consistency is reminiscent of the great DiMaggio. In 1999, he set a team record by reaching base in each of the first fifty-three games of the season.

While continuing to add individual honors, such as the 2004 and 2005 Gold Glove awards, Jeter manages to lead the team at the same time.

"I'm very proud of Derek Jeter," Steinbrenner said. "He's a great leader and a great captain, and he deserves every honor he wins. He truly works hard for the Yankees and for our fans."[5]

Jeter strokes a single against the Angels October 4, 2005.

CAREER STATISTICS

SEASON	G	AB	R	H	2B	3B
1995	15	48	5	12	4	1
1996	157	582	104	183	25	6
1997	159	654	116	190	31	7
1998	149	626	127	203	25	8
1999	158	627	134	219	37	9
2000	148	593	119	201	31	4
2001	150	614	110	191	35	3
2002	157	644	124	191	26	0
2003	119	482	87	156	25	3
2004	154	643	111	188	44	1
2005	159	654	122	202	25	5
2006	154	623	118	214	39	3
2007	156	639	102	206	39	4
2008	150	596	88	179	25	3
CAREER	1,985	8,025	1,467	2,535	411	57

KEY:
G – Games
AB – At Bats
R – Runs Scored
H – Hits
2B – Doubles
3B – Triples
HR – Home Runs

RBI – Runs Batted In
BB – Bases on Balls (walks)
SO – Strikeouts
SB – Stolen Bases
CS – Caught Stealing
AVG – Batting Average

HR	RBI	BB	SO	SB	CS	AVG
0	7	3	11	0	0	.250
10	78	48	102	14	7	.314
10	70	74	125	23	12	.291
19	84	57	119	30	6	.324
24	102	91	116	19	8	.349
15	73	68	99	22	4	.339
21	74	56	99	27	3	.311
18	75	73	114	32	3	.297
10	52	43	88	11	5	.324
23	78	46	99	23	4	.292
19	70	77	117	14	5	.309
14	97	69	102	34	5	.343
12	73	56	100	15	8	.322
11	69	52	85	11	5	.300
206	1,002	813	1,376	275	75	.316

CAREER ACHIEVEMENTS

1992	Named High School Player of the Year
June 1992	Sixth overall draft pick and first high school player chosen in baseball draft
1994	Named Minor League Player of the Year
May 29, 1995	Makes Major League debut, playing shortstop for the New York Yankees in Seattle
April 1996	First rookie to be Opening Day shortstop for the Yankees since Tom Tresh in 1962
October 1996	Batted .361 in postseason to help Yankees win their first World Series since 1978
November 5, 1996	Named American League Rookie of the Year by a unanimous vote
1996	Creates the Turn 2 Foundation
1998	Helps Yankees win World Series
1998	Finishes third in American League Most Valuable Player voting

October 18, 1999   Hits home run in American League Championship Series—clinching victory over the Boston Red Sox and Yankees go on to win World Series

1999   Finishes sixth in American League Most Valuable Player voting after hitting .349 with 24 homers and 102 RBIs

2000   Named All-Star Game Most Valuable Player after going 3-for-3

October 26, 2000   Named Most Valuable Player of World Series after hitting .407 in five-game win over New York Mets

October 31, 2001   Hits game-winning home run in 10th inning of Game 4 of World Series against Arizona Diamondbacks

June 3, 2003   Named captain of the Yankees

July, 2004   Goes 3-for-3 in All-Star Game for second time in career

October 2005   Hits 2 home runs in five games, but Yankees are eliminated in American League Divisional Series

CHAPTER NOTES

CHAPTER 1. THRIVING IN THE SPOTLIGHT

1. Derek Jeter, with Jack Curry, *The Life You Imagine: Life Lessons for Achieving Your Dreams* (New York: Three Rivers Press, 2000), p. 225.

2. John Lowe, "Rookie Jeter Pleased in Pinstripes—Parents Watch Kalamazoo Shortstop Make Major Step with Yanks," *Detroit Free Press,* April 2, 1996.

CHAPTER 2. FAMILY INFLUENCE

1. Derek Jeter, with Jack Curry, *The Life You Imagine: Life Lessons for Achieving Your Dreams* (New York: Three Rivers Press, 2000), p. 87.

2. Ibid., p. 149.

3. "Derek Jeter Gives Kids Someone to Turn 2," MLB Web site, http://derekjeter.mlb.com/NASApp/mlb/players/jeter_derek/turn2/turn2 us.jsp (December 9, 2005).

4. Ibid.

CHAPTER 3. PREPARING EARLY

1. Derek Jeter, with Jack Curry, *The Life You Imagine: Life Lessons for Achieving Your Dreams* (New York: Three Rivers Press, 2000), p. 110.

2. Ibid., p. 111.

CHAPTER 4. SOMEBODY IS WATCHING

1. Derek Jeter, with Jack Curry, *The Life You Imagine: Life Lessons for Achieving Your Dreams* (New York: Three Rivers Press, 2000), p. 47.

CHAPTER 5. MOMENTS OF DOUBT

1. Derek Jeter, with Jack Curry, *The Life You Imagine: Life Lessons for Achieving Your Dreams* (New York: Three Rivers Press, 2000), pp. 24-25.

2. Ibid., pp. 12-13.

3. Ibid., p. 35.

4. Jon Heyman, "Jeter's Next Job May be Shortstop at the Stadium," *New York Newsday*, August 18, 1994.

CHAPTER 6. ON THE RISE

1. Jon Heyman, "Jeter's Next Job May be Shortstop at the Stadium," *New York Newsday*, August 18, 1994.

2. David Lennon, "Long Term at Short – Youngsters Ready to Provide Excitement at an Important Position," *New York Newsday*, April 3, 1996.

CHAPTER 7. CHAMPIONSHIP FEELING

1. "Metro golden Maier," *New York Daily News* Web site, April 15, 2003. <http://www.nydailynews.com/sports/baseball/story/75709p-69921c.html> (December 1, 2005).

2. Tom Verducci. "Stroke of Fate: As New York rallied to win four straight games from Atlanta, its World Series title seemed preordained," World Series archives, *Sports Illustrated* Web site, November 4, 1996. <http://sportsillustrated.cnn.com/baseball/mlb/features/1997/wsarchive/1996.html> (December 1, 2005).

3. Ibid.

4. Derek Jeter, with Jack Curry, *The Life You Imagine: Life Lessons for Achieving Your Dreams* (New York: Three Rivers Press, 2000), p. 20.

CHAPTER 8. TURNING TWO

1. Derek Jeter Gives Kids Someone to Turn 2. MLB Web site, http://derek-jeter.mlb.com/NASApp/mlb/players/jeter_derek/turn2/turn2us.jsp (December 9, 2005).

2. Derek Jeter, with Jack Curry, *The Life You Imagine: Life Lessons for Achieving Your Dreams* (New York: Three Rivers Press, 2000), pp. 210-211.

3. "Statement from Derek Jeter regarding 2005 Gold Glove," Press release, November 1, 2005. New York Yankees Web site. http://newyork.yankees.mlb.com/NASApp/mlb/news/press_releases/press_release.jsp?ymd=20051101&content_id=1263360&vkey=pr_nyy&fext=.jsp&c_id=nyy (December 9, 2005).

CHAPTER 9. MR. CLUTCH

1. Michael Knisley, "History of the World Series – 2000," *The Sporting News* Web site. <http://www.sportingnews.com/archives/world-series/2000.html> (December 2, 2005).

2. Michael Knisley, "History of the World Series – 1999," *The Sporting News* Web site. <http://www.sportingnews.com/archives/world-series/1999.html> (December 2, 2005).

3. "Sports Illustrated's Derek Jeter Scrapbook: Timeline," *Sports Illustrated* Web site, October 1, 2002 (December 2, 2005).

4. Ibid.

CHAPTER 10. THE CAPTAIN

1. Anthony McCarron, "Jeter gets 'C', in Cincinnati?: Time & place for honor raise questions," *New York Daily News,* June 4, 2003.

2. Ibid.

3. "Shortstop follows in footsteps of Ruth, Gehrig," Associated Press story on *ESPN.com* Web site, June 3, 2003. <espn.go.com/mlb/news/2003/0603/1562514.html> (December 3, 2005).

4. Anthony McCarron, "Jeter gets 'C', in Cincinnati?: Time & place for honor raise questions," *New York Daily News*, June 4, 2003.

5. Mark Feinsand, "Jeter wins second straight Gold Glove: Shortstop lone Yankees winner; A-Rod beaten out by Chavez," New York Yankees Web site, November 1, 2005. http://newyork.yankees.mlb.com/NASApp/mlb/news/article.jsp?ymd=20051101&content_id=1263171&vkey=news_nyy&fext=.jsp&c_id=nyy (December 9, 2005).

GLOSSARY

captain—A member of a sports team who is recognized as the leader.

charity—The act of giving or an organization that gives to the needy.

counselor—A person who gives advice as a profession.

draft—A process in which professional sports teams choose players in order.

error—A misplay on defense that allows a batter to be safe or a runner to advance to another base.

farm system—The use by Major League Baseball teams of lower-level teams designed to develop talent.

general manager—The person responsible for organizing a professional sports team, including making trades and signing players to contracts.

manager—The head coach of a professional baseball team.

prospect—An athlete who is believed to have the potential to perform on a higher level.

rookie—A first-year professional.

scholarship—A grant of money to a student for educational purposes; top athletes are offered scholarships by colleges to attend and play sports for their schools.

scouts—People who evaluate baseball players to help teams determine who to draft and/or sign to contracts.

shortstop—A defensive position in baseball where the player usually lines up on the left side (third-base side) of the infield, close to second base.

spring training—When baseball teams travel to Florida or Arizona to prepare for an upcoming season.

total bases—The number of bases gained on hits; a single counts as one total base, a double as two, a triple as three, and a home run as four.

World Series—A series of between four and seven games, matching the American League and National League baseball champions. The first team to win four games is declared world champion.

FOR MORE INFORMATION

FURTHER READING

Derek Jeter: A Yankee for the New Millennium. Dallas: Beckett Publications, 2000.

Jeter, Derek. *Derek Jeter, Game Day: My Life On and Off the Field.* New York: Three Rivers Press, 2001.

Jeter, Derek, with Jack Curry. *The Life You Imagine: Life Lessons for Achieving Your Dreams.* New York: Three Rivers Press, 2000.

WEB LINKS

Turn 2
http://derekjeter.mlb.com/NASApp/mlb/players/
jeter_derek/turn2/index.jsp

Jeter's page on MLB.com
http://newyork.yankees.mlb.com/team/player.jsp?player_id=
116539

Jeter's page on ESPN Web site
http://sports.espn.go.com/mlb/players/profile?statsId=5406

Jeter's page on Baseball-Reference.com
http://www.baseball-reference.com/j/jeterde01.shtml

INDEX

E

ESPY, 6, 8

F

Fernandez, Tony, 50, 51

Florida Marlins, 107

Florida State League, 46, 48

G

Garcia, Rich, 62

Gehrig, Lou, 12, 93, 103, 109, 110

Giambi, Jeremy, 5, 6

Gold Glove, 8, 70, 79, 81, 110

Gonzalez, Luis, 106

Groch, Dick, 33, 46

Gulf Coast League, 38

H

Hayes, Charlie, 67

I

Instructional League, 44

J

K

L

Lemke, Mark, 67

Leyritz, Jim, 64, 65, 68

Los Angeles Dodgers, 28, 59, 60

M

Maier, Jeffrey, 60, 62

Mantle, Mickey, 86, 93

Maris, Roger, 93

Martinez, Tino, 92

Mattingly, Don, 10–11, 81, 103, 109

Michael, Gene, 44

Munson, Thurman, 56, 81, 103, 109

N

New York Giants, 59, 82

New York Mets, 35, 67, 82–84, 87, 96, 98

New York Yankees

    scouting Derek Jeter, 32, 33, 46

    signing Derek Jeter, 36, 38

Nixon, Trot, 87

O

Oakland Athletics, 5–6, 57, 59, 89, 95, 96, 98

O'Neill, Paul, 93

W